Original title:
Thread of Hope

Copyright © 2024 Creative Arts Management OÜ
All rights reserved.

Author: Colin Leclair
ISBN HARDBACK: 978-9916-90-824-2
ISBN PAPERBACK: 978-9916-90-825-9

Infinite Stitches

In a world of fabric and thread,
Each stitch connects heart to soul.
Patterns emerge, brightly spread,
Stories unfold, making us whole.

Yarns of wisdom woven tight,
Colors of love, bold and true.
Infinite stitches, pure delight,
Crafting a life, made anew.

Embroidered Paths

Paths adorned with vibrant hues,
Every step, a tale to trace.
Embroidered dreams, old and new,
Guiding us through time and space.

Winding roads with sparkle bound,
Journeys stitched with care and grace.
In each thread, the love we found,
Leading us in our embrace.

Patterns of Strength

In the weave, a tale of might,
Strength is stitched within the seams.
Patterns formed through day and night,
Resilience born from hopeful dreams.

Together we can face the storm,
With hands united, side by side.
In every shape, a brighter form,
Our patterns blend, our spirits ride.

Unbroken Threads

Threads of fate, unbroken, strong,
Binding us in harmony.
Through the trials, we belong,
Stitching our own destiny.

In the fabric of our lives,
Every line holds strength defined.
Together, hope forever thrives,
In unbroken threads, love aligned.

Embroidery of Belief

In shadows deep, we stitch our dreams,
Fingers dance on life's soft seams.
Threads of hope woven tight,
Crafting dawn from endless night.

Each knot a promise softly sewn,
With every tear, our spirits grown.
Patterns bright in life's vast scheme,
We trace the edges of our dream.

The Loom of New Beginnings

The loom awaits, its fibers bare,
A canvas clean, a breath of air.
New colors blend, old fades away,
In this moment, we find our way.

Each pull of thread, a step anew,
Woven tales within the blue.
With patience learned from earth and sky,
We craft the fabric of our why.

Fragments of a Rising Sun

Morning breaks, the world in gold,
Scattered pieces, stories told.
Soft whispers of the night retreat,
As light ignites the day's heartbeat.

The sun ascends, a painter's brush,
Coloring life in every hush.
Shattered remnants find their place,
In the glow, we find our grace.

Colors of a Restored Heart

In shades of love, the heart regains,
The vibrant hues that ease its pains.
Each pulse a stroke, each beat a part,
The canvas blooms with a fresh start.

Restoration whispers sweet and low,
Bringing warmth, where once was woe.
In the spectrum of our truth, we find,
The beauty woven, heart aligned.

The Stitch That Binds

In threads of hope we find our place,
With every knot, we weave with grace.
Together stitched through thick and thin,
Our hearts entwined, a bond within.

Through storms and trials, we hold tight,
A tapestry of shared delight.
With every stitch, love's stories blend,
In the fabric of life, we transcend.

Fibers of Unyielding Spirit

Strong as the roots of ancient trees,
Our spirit bends but does not seize.
Each thread of courage tightly spun,
In unity, we shine like the sun.

In shadows deep, our light remains,
Resilient hearts through joy and pains.
Together we rise, never apart,
With fibers woven from the heart.

Unraveling Doubt

In moments dark when fears take flight,
We seek the dawn to bring back light.
Each question posed, a thread pulled tight,
In unraveling, we find our sight.

With patience learned, we face the haze,
In clarity's warmth, we find our ways.
Through tangled paths, we journey on,
In strength reborn, our doubts are gone.

Blessings in the Weave

In patterns bright, our stories blend,
Each twist a joy, each loop a friend.
We find the beauty in design,
With blessings rich in every line.

Through layers thick, our hopes entwined,
In this great tapestry, we're aligned.
With every thread a gift we share,
In love's embrace, we find our prayer.

Ties that Bind

In silent moments, we find our grace,
Threads of connection, time can't erase.
Through laughter and tears, we weave our song,
In the tapestry of life, we all belong.

Hands held tightly, hearts open wide,
Shadows may linger, but love is our guide.
Together we stand, facing the test,
In this dance of life, we are truly blessed.

Fabric of the Future

Woven with dreams, each thread a story,
Colors of hope in all their glory.
Stitches of courage, bold and bright,
Crafting tomorrow with passion and light.

Patterns emerging, unique and new,
Crafted by hands that dare to pursue.
In every fold, potential is sewn,
A future united, together we've grown.

Starlit Pathways

Under a blanket of shimmering skies,
Guided by stars, where the universe lies.
Each step we take, a dance of delight,
Exploring the dreams that shine through the night.

Whispers of cosmos, echoing near,
Paths intertwined, as we journey here.
With hearts full of wonder, we chase the dawn,
On starlit pathways, our souls are reborn.

Twists and Turns of Fate

Life's winding roads, with surprises untold,
Moments of magic, and stories bold.
With each twist, a lesson unfolds,
In the hands of fate, we find our gold.

Choices we make, like rivers flow wide,
Carving our futures, with courage and pride.
In the dance of life, we embrace the sway,
Navigating fate, come what may.

Fibers of Joy

In morning light, we weave so bright,
A tapestry of dreams in flight.
Each smile is stitched, each laugh a thread,
In the fabric of life, where love is spread.

With colors bold, we blend our fears,
Crafting happiness through the years.
Each joy a knot, secure and tight,
In the heart's embrace, we find our light.

Threads of Tomorrow

With whispers soft, the future calls,
A woven path where courage sprawls.
Each moment holds a promise near,
In the dreamer's heart, we conquer fear.

Threads of hope entwine our fate,
In every stitch, we create the great.
The fabric stretches, yet holds so strong,
In unity and love, we all belong.

Chains of Tomorrow

Links of fate, one by one,
Together they shine, like the sun.
Bound by visions, we rise anew,
In the chains of tomorrow, dreams come true.

Each link a story, forged with care,
In the heart's workshop, we lay them bare.
A chorus of voices, loud and free,
In this chain of life, we find our key.

Woven Aspirations

In the loom of hope, we spin our thread,
Turning aspirations into dreams ahead.
Each loom a story, unique and true,
Crafting the future, me and you.

With every twist, our visions grow,
In vibrant hues, our spirits flow.
Woven together, we rise and stand,
Creating a world, woven hand in hand.

The Fabric of Endurance

Through storms we stand, we weave our dreams,
With threads of hope, like sunlight beams.
In darkest nights, we find our way,
Resilient hearts, come what may.

Each stitch a promise, each knot a tie,
We rise again, we learn to fly.
With every tear, we mend and bind,
In woven strength, our truths we find.

Threads of a Brighter Day

With morning light, new paths we see,
Our hearts entwined, we choose to be.
The colors dance in gentle sway,
We craft our lives, come what may.

Amid the shadows, brilliance glows,
In every laugh, the joy just flows.
Together we stitch a vibrant ray,
For hope is born in our array.

Sewing Seeds of Joy

In gardens green, we plant our bliss,
With tender hands, we nurture this.
Each seed a wish, a dream in flight,
We cultivate love, day and night.

As blossoms bloom, our hearts align,
In fragrant air, our spirits shine.
With every smile, joy takes its place,
In life's embrace, we find our grace.

Patterns of Faith

In woven dreams, we seek the light,
With faith as thread, we soar to heights.
Each prayer a stitch, a sacred space,
In patterns bold, we find our grace.

Through trials faced, we hold it close,
In shared moments, we find our dose.
With every heartbeat, love will stay,
In life's fabric, we choose our way.

Interwoven Wishes

In the fabric of dreams we weave,
Threads of light, a soft reprieve.
Colors blend in twilight's glow,
Hopes and wishes start to flow.

Each stitch a promise, pure and bright,
Embracing shadows, bringing light.
Together we create this tapestry,
A world of dreams, wild and free.

Through the loom of time, we write,
Whispers echo, day and night.
Hands unite, as hearts align,
In every thread, our souls entwine.

Patchwork of Tomorrow's Promise

A patchwork quilt of futures bold,
Stories woven, dreams retold.
Each square a vision, bright and new,
Crafted with hope, stitched with rue.

Colors dancing, hands at play,
In every seam, the light of day.
Threads of laughter, tears entwined,
Healing hearts, two souls aligned.

As we gather all our fears,
Knot them tightly, share our years.
In this quilt of tomorrow's grace,
A patchwork journey, love's embrace.

A Stitch in Time

A stitch in time, a gentle thread,
Binds our moments, softly spread.
With needle poised and heart's intent,
We shape the path where love is meant.

Through trials faced, we mend the seams,
Repairing hopes, igniting dreams.
Each thread we pull, a story told,
In the tapestry, bold and gold.

Time may fray, yet here we stand,
Hand in hand, we understand.
Stitch by stitch, our lives align,
Crafting fate, a design divine.

Whispers of the Unseen

In the silence, whispers rise,
Echoing softly beneath the skies.
Unseen forces guide our way,
Through hidden paths, we choose to stray.

With every breath, a secret shared,
In shadows deep, our hearts bared.
Hand in hand, we dare to trust,
Beyond the veil, it's love that must.

In the night, stars weave and spin,
A dance of fate, where dreams begin.
Listen closely, for they sing,
Of whispers soft, the light they bring.

Patchwork of Tomorrow

In fragments bright and bold,
We stitch the days to come.
Each patch a story told,
In hues of hope, we hum.

With threads of love entwined,
We craft a future clear.
In every shade, we find
The dreams we hold so dear.

A quilt of every heart,
Woven with threads of grace.
Together, not apart,
We shape our sacred space.

So let the needles dance,
With every guiding hand.
In this bright, bold expanse,
We weave our promised land.

The Yarn of Potential

A single strand unfolds,
Endless paths await.
In fibers soft, we hold,
The dreams we cultivate.

With every gentle twist,
A vision starts to grow.
In shadows, light will kiss
The seeds we dare to sow.

Each loop a chance embraced,
To rise above the fray.
In whispers, hope is laced,
As we find our own way.

With colors yet unspooled,
The canvas waits in peace.
In potential, we're ruled,
As fears begin to cease.

Knots of Encouragement

In tangled threads we find,
A bond that will not break.
With each supportive line,
We gain the strength to take.

When doubts begin to swell,
We tie a sturdy knot.
With every loving yell,
We step from fear and rot.

Together we will rise,
Unraveled by our cheer.
In every heart, the prize
Is knowing we are here.

So let us weave this strength,
In courage's embrace.
With bonds of love at length,
We stand in hope's bright grace.

Woven Dreams

In twilight's gentle glow,
We cast a net of light.
With every thread in tow,
Our dreams take shape tonight.

Each vision, finely spun,
A tapestry so grand.
Beneath the setting sun,
We weave what we have planned.

As stars begin to shine,
Our hopes reflect the sky.
With every strand, we climb,
To reach where dreams can fly.

In unity, we stand,
Our hearts, a vibrant scene.
Together, hand in hand,
We weave the life we dream.

Fabricated Resilience

In shadows cast by doubt's cold hand,
We weave our dreams in a fragile strand.
Each thread a promise, barely spun,
Yet strong enough to face the sun.

With every knot, we mend the seams,
Resilient hearts, alive with dreams.
Through storms we stand, unbowed, unshaken,
In this tapestry, joy is awakened.

Embroidered Futures

With needle poised, we sketch the night,
Embroidering futures, bold and bright.
Each stitch a story waiting to unfold,
In vibrant patterns, new and old.

We gather hopes like threads untwined,
In every loop, a spark, defined.
Together we craft a life unique,
With colors rich, the future speaks.

Unraveling Joy

In woven fields of laughter's grace,
We find our joy in every space.
Unraveling moments, fleeting, sweet,
In simple threads, our hearts repeat.

With every pull, the laughter spills,
In warm embrace, our spirit thrills.
We dance through life with threads of gold,
In joy's embrace, let life unfold.

Belief in Every Stitch

In every stitch, we plant our faith,
A tapestry of hope, our wraith.
With careful hands, we craft the light,
Believing in dreams that take to flight.

Each knot a prayer, held tight and strong,
In this woven world, we belong.
Together we bind the moments near,
In every stitch, we conquer fear.

Journey of the Heart

In the stillness of dawn's light,
Footsteps echo, soft and bright.
Paths unworn call out the brave,
Hearts awaken, dreams to save.

Through valleys deep and mountains high,
Love's compass guides as we fly.
Every turn a new surprise,
The journey leads to open skies.

Embers of Promise

In the glow of twilight's hue,
Whispers linger, soft and true.
Each ember holds a tale untold,
Promises warm, a sight to behold.

As shadows dance, hopes ignite,
Futures flicker in the night.
Together we'll fan the flame,
For love's embers call our name.

Unseen Connections

Threads invisible intertwine,
Binding souls in space and time.
In a glance, a heartbeat shared,
Unseen bonds that showed we cared.

With every laugh, with every tear,
Distance fades when love is near.
In silence speaks the heart's retreat,
Connections carved in moments sweet.

Weaving the Unknown

With hands of fate, we stitch and sew,
Patterns made from what we know.
Each thread a dream, a wish, a fear,
In the tapestry, we draw near.

The loom of time spins tales anew,
The unknown calls, a vibrant hue.
In every twist, in every turn,
Wisdom gained, and passions burn.

Motley Hues of Hope

In the dawn of a brand new day,
Colors blend in a vibrant array.
Dreams are stitched with threads so fine,
Bringing warmth like the sun that shines.

Each hue whispers a tale untold,
A promise wrapped in dappled gold.
Through shadows cast by doubt's embrace,
Hope's palette paints a brighter place.

In every struggle, a spark ignites,
Motley hues dance in joyful flights.
Beneath the clouds, a rainbow gleams,
Woven tightly into our dreams.

Together we rise, hands intertwined,
With every heartbeat, our paths aligned.
Through motley hues of love and trust,
We discover strength, as we must.

Threads of Light

In the quiet of the fading night,
A whisper weaves with threads of light.
Stars shimmer softly, guiding the way,
Illuminating hopes that refuse to sway.

Through the fabric of dreams we traverse,
Each thread holds promise, a universe.
Woven together, our stories unite,
Creating a tapestry, pure and bright.

With each stitch, a moment defined,
Embracing the journey, hearts intertwined.
Threads of courage, spun from the heart,
In darkness and doubt, we find our part.

As dawn approaches, shadows retreat,
In the warmth of the day, we find our beat.
Threads of light, a radiant gleam,
Together we chase our shared dream.

Designs of Tomorrow

Upon the canvas of days to come,
Ideas flourish, a hopeful hum.
Each sketch a glimpse of what may be,
In dreams we weave our destiny.

Lines are drawn with purpose and care,
Crafting visions that dance in the air.
Imagination blooms, a vibrant seed,
In the soil of thought, we plant the need.

From whispers born of quiet nights,
Creation sparks, igniting lights.
With every brush and every pen,
Tomorrow designs itself again.

As we stand on the brink of change,
Embracing paths that feel so strange.
In the art of living, we find our way,
Designs of tomorrow start today.

The Warped Loom

Threads entangle in a mystic weave,
A tale of life that we conceive.
The loom may twist and turn in pain,
Yet beauty surfaces through the strain.

Patterns form in chaotic dance,
Life's intricacies play their chance.
With each loop, a story bends,
In the warp and weft, the journey sends.

We gather strength from fibers worn,
In the fabric of sorrow, hope is born.
The loom may strain, but it won't break,
With every stitch, new paths we make.

Embrace the flaws, the knots and tears,
The warped loom holds all our cares.
Through tangled threads, our hearts align,
In love's great fabric, we find the design.

Crafted by Faith

In the quiet whispers of the night,
Hands shape the dreams, taking flight.
With threads of hope, we weave our way,
In shadows and light, we find our stay.

Through trials faced, we learn to bend,
With every stitch, our hearts we mend.
In patterns formed, our stories told,
By faith and love, we break the mold.

From tangled fears, new strength begins,
With every loss, the spirit wins.
Crafted by hands that know their place,
Life's tapestry is woven with grace.

With faith as the guide, we chart the course,
In every stitch, we find our source.
Together we craft, together we dream,
In a world of wonders, we gleam.

Interlaced Wishes

Woven together, wishes align,
In the fabric of life, we find the sign.
Threads of laughter, tears set free,
In every moment, we cease to be.

With each gentle tug, hearts undress,
Interlaced dreams in a soft caress.
Patterns emerging, unseen at first,
In hope's embrace, our spirits thirst.

Amidst the noise, whispers abound,
In the silence, our truths are found.
With every knot that binds us tight,
Wishes take wing, claiming their flight.

As colors blend into the night,
Interwoven paths reveal the light.
Through tapestry, we dance and sway,
Our interlaced wishes lead the way.

New Patterns Unfolding

In the loom of time, new patterns weave,
With each sunrise, we dare to believe.
Threads of moments, varying in hue,
In every choice, we start anew.

Patterns shifting like the whispering sea,
Change is the art of what's meant to be.
In the dance of colors, we find our ground,
As new horizons rise from the profound.

With every twist, a chance to create,
In the fabric of life, we celebrate fate.
Together we grow, in harmony's sway,
New patterns forming with each passing day.

In the gentle hands of tomorrow's dawn,
Hope interlaces, and fears are gone.
We embrace the journey, both wild and bold,
In new patterns unfolding, our story is told.

The Needle's Journey

The needle glides through fabric and thread,
In the dance of creation, dreams are bred.
With every pull, a story is spun,
In the hands of time, the journey begun.

Through stitches small, we mend the rift,
A tender embrace, life's precious gift.
In every loop, connections are made,
A tapestry rich, never to fade.

The needle's journey, both bold and kind,
In its simple path, the heart aligned.
With every knot, we find our way,
In the quilt of existence, come what may.

So hold the thread and guide it through,
Embrace each moment, let love renew.
For the needle's journey is ours to take,
In every creation, new bonds we make.

Vibrant Connections

In the dance of light and shade,
Colors merge in soft cascade.
Whispers echo, hearts align,
In this moment, you are mine.

Joy spills over like the sun,
Unity where two are one.
Hands entwined across the space,
Finding warmth in every trace.

Infinity Stitched

Threads of fate, they pull and weave,
Patterns form, we dare believe.
In the tapestry of time,
Endless echoes, a silent chime.

Each knot tied with hopes anew,
Infinite stories coming through.
Boundless dreams in every stitch,
Life's rich fabric, love's true pitch.

Weaving the Unseen

In shadows where the silence breathes,
Unseen bonds a heart deceives.
We gather fragments, each a piece,
Creating beauty, finding peace.

With every thread, a story spun,
Hidden pathways, journeys run.
In the fabric of the night,
The unseen glimmers, soft and bright.

The Journey of Threads

Along the path where fibers blend,
Each mile traversed, a welcoming friend.
Twists and turns in vibrant hue,
We stitch our dreams in shades anew.

With every loop, a tale unfolds,
In whispered patterns, courage holds.
The journey calls with each new day,
As threads unite in bright display.

Tapestry of Tomorrow

Threads of gold weave brighter days,
Whispers of hope in sunlit rays.
Dreams entwined, they softly soar,
Crafting futures on the shore.

Fingers dance on fabric wide,
Nestled hopes that coincide.
Every knot a promise made,
In this art, our fears do fade.

Colors blend, as visions twine,
With every stitch, the stars align.
Together we'll unfurl our dreams,
The tapestry in vibrant beams.

Time will pass, yet still we stand,
Stitching fate with steady hand.
For in this craft, we find our way,
Tomorrow's light shall guide our play.

A Stitch in Time

A needle glints in morning's glow,
Each stitch holds tales of long ago.
Moments captured, threads entwined,
In fabric hearts, the past aligned.

The tapestry, it bends and sways,
Guiding us through life's long maze.
With every flick, a promise sewn,
Memories linger, love is known.

In patterns forged, we find our peace,
A stitch in time, our doubts release.
Binding stories, hopes, and dreams,
A healing quilt from all it seems.

Beneath the stars, our dreams will soar,
In threads of love we'll weave once more.
Each moment cherished, each lesson learned,
With every stitch, our hearts returned.

Colors of the Heart

A palette rich, our spirits dance,
With shades of love, we take a chance.
Crimson joys and azure tears,
Brush strokes blend through hopes and fears.

Emerald whispers fill the air,
Each hue a tale, a song, a prayer.
Violet dreams and golden light,
Together paint the endless night.

In bursts of color, we unite,
Creating art in darkest night.
With every tone, our stories bloom,
A symphony to chase the gloom.

Let passion flow like rivers wide,
In every shade, let love abide.
For when we blend, a masterpiece,
The colors of the heart bring peace.

The Loom of Change

In quiet corners, shadows play,
The loom of change, it calls today.
Tread softly on the threads of fate,
As moments weave and hearts elate.

Cycles turn and colors shift,
In every loss, a hidden gift.
From silver strands to darkest hue,
A tapestry of all that's true.

With every revolution spun,
The fabric stretches, lives begun.
Transformation weaves in every line,
In changing winds, our hopes align.

Let passion guide each gentle hand,
Embrace the change, together stand.
As threads entwine, we'll rise anew,
Creating dreams, both bright and true.

Canvas of Possibilities

Upon the canvas, colors spread,
Imagination dances, softly fed.
Brush strokes whisper tales untold,
In vibrant hues, our dreams unfold.

Each stroke a choice, a path we see,
Crafting moments, wild and free.
A tapestry of hopes and fears,
In every layer, time appears.

Gold and azure, red and green,
The beauty lies in what's between.
Every splatter, a chance to grow,
A canvas rich with all we know.

So wield the brush, let visions rise,
In this vast world, be ever wise.
For on this canvas, life's a dream,
A masterpiece, a radiant beam.

Laced with Dreams

Threads of hope intertwine and weave,
In the fabric of night, we believe.
Stitch by stitch, the stories flow,
Patterns formed in soft moon's glow.

Whispers of wishes dance with light,
Each laced dream ignites the night.
Woven tight with love and care,
A tapestry of thoughts laid bare.

Ribbons curl like winds of fate,
Sewing together what love creates.
In every seam, a secret lies,
A patchwork quilt of silent sighs.

Embroidered hopes, a bright embrace,
In this warm quilt, we find our place.
Bound by dreams and threads so fine,
A life enriched, a joyful design.

The Journey of Yarn

A single thread, a winding road,
From spool to fabric, stories flowed.
Every twist, a path to tread,
In the warmth of love, we're led.

Knitting hearts with every row,
Stitching time as moments glow.
Through ups and downs, the rhythm beats,
In this journey, life repeats.

Colors blend like laughter's song,
Each loop and purl, a tale so strong.
Crafting memories, warm and bright,
Beneath the stars, we find our light.

Let's weave together dreams so grand,
With gentle hands, let's take a stand.
For in this yarn, our hopes take flight,
A tapestry woven through the night.

Echoes of Tomorrow

Soft whispers drift on breezes light,
Carrying dreams into the night.
In shadows deep, our hopes will gleam,
Echoes of tomorrow, the seeds we dream.

Each moment fleeting, yet it stays,
In silent echoes, love displays.
The past and future in harmony blend,
Guiding our steps, a faithful friend.

Let new horizons call our names,
In the dance of time, we play our games.
With every heartbeat, the future sings,
In echoes of tomorrow, hope takes wings.

Through valleys low and mountains high,
We chase the stars, beneath the sky.
For every echo holds a light,
Leading us onward, into the night.

The Fabric of Belief

Threads intertwine, colors bright,
Woven dreams in the soft light,
Whispers of hope, secrets kept,
In the loom of the heart, love is adept.

Tattered edges hint at strife,
Yet strengthen the weave of life,
Every fiber holds a tale,
In this tapestry, none shall fail.

Stitch by stitch, we create our way,
Through shadows of doubt, fears at bay,
The fabric stretches, yet remains,
In the hands of those who sustain.

Belief is the thread, strong and bold,
In the warm embrace, stories unfold,
As we gather under the great sky,
United in faith, we learn to fly.

Unraveled Possibilities

Threads lie scattered on the ground,
Dreams unspooled, without a sound,
In the chaos, paths may hide,
Waiting for courage to decide.

What if we weave anew each day?
Embrace the mess, let go, and play,
In uncertainty, beauty thrives,
Unraveled paths lead to new lives.

With every knot comes a new chance,
To dance in the wild, to take a stance,
The frayed edges tell of each fall,
Yet from them, we rise, we stand tall.

Possibilities whisper and call,
Inviting us to break down the wall,
In the fabric of dreams set free,
Together we shape our destiny.

Silk of Resilience

Soft and strong, a silken thread,
Woven through trials, tears we shed,
Draped in warmth, we find our way,
Through storms that dare to lead us astray.

With every twist, a lesson learned,
In the fire of life, our spirits burned,
Yet, like silk, we shimmer and glow,
Resilience springs from the depths below.

Threads of hope bound tight with care,
In the weave of life, we find what's rare,
Through every tear, we mend and sew,
Stitching together what we must grow.

Silk of resilience, shining bright,
Guides us through the longest night,
Embracing each challenge with grace,
We rise anew, a stronger embrace.

Needle of Faith

A needle glimmers in the sun,
Through fabric of dreams, it swiftly runs,
With each pull, we craft our fate,
Sewing together love and hate.

Faith is the thread that holds us near,
Through every doubt and shadowed fear,
In the heart's work, we find our way,
A guiding light within the fray.

Stitch by stitch, we build our trust,
In the needle's eye, our hopes adjust,
Joining hands across the seams,
In the threads of faith, we weave our dreams.

With each stitch, a story told,
In the tapestry, our hearts unfold,
The needle of faith, so subtle and strong,
In the fabric of life, we all belong.

Loom of Destiny

In shadows cast by fate's design,
Threads intertwine, both yours and mine.
Each movement brings a tale untold,
Woven tight, in dreams we hold.

The shuttle flies, the tension lifts,
In every weave, a life adrift.
Patterns shift like whispered sighs,
In the loom, our future lies.

Colors clash and harmonize,
In this dance, where fortune lies.
The weaver's hand, so wise and bold,
Shapes our paths in threads of gold.

As we stand on edges near,
The loom spins forth, dissolving fear.
With every knot, our hearts expand,
Together now, we take a stand.

Bright Threads in the Dark

In the vast abyss of midnight's cloak,
Bright threads shimmer, softly spoke.
A gentle light in shadow's snare,
Guiding us with tender care.

Each needle's prick, a spark ignites,
Hope emerges in the lonely nights.
Stitched together, the memories gleam,
A tapestry woven from the dream.

Through storms we sail, through darkest fears,
With every stitch, we dry our tears.
The threads unite in colors bold,
Creating warmth against the cold.

In the dark, we find our way,
Bright threads leading as we sway.
United in this woven art,
Together strong, we'll never part.

Seamstress of Wishes

She stitches dreams with gentle care,
Whispers woven in the air.
With every wish, a needle's kiss,
Creating magic, a simple bliss.

The fabric holds our deepest hopes,
In every thread, a world elopes.
Silken strands of bright desire,
Filling hearts with vibrant fire.

The seamstress hums a lullaby,
While fabric dances, spirits fly.
Each stitch a promise, soft yet strong,
In her embrace, you can't go wrong.

As wishes float like clouds above,
She weaves them in, a tale of love.
In every seam, a dream takes flight,
Guided by her gentle light.

Stitching Together Hope

With every knot, we heal the pain,
Stitching hope where loss remains.
Through frayed edges, new starts bloom,
In the silence, dispelling gloom.

Patchwork hearts, sewn with belief,
Binding strength amid the grief.
Each color chosen, a tale unfolds,
In the fabric, our courage holds.

Threads of kindness intertwine,
Connect our stories through design.
Woven tightly, a shared embrace,
In this tapestry, we find our place.

As needles glide, we rise anew,
Stitching together, me and you.
In every seam, a future bright,
In this quilt of hope, we find our light.

Weaving Light in Shadows

In the twilight's gentle embrace,
Threads of hope begin to trace.
Flickers dance in muted night,
Shadows weave the fabric bright.

Whispers carried on the breeze,
Secrets told among the trees.
Every thread a story spun,
In this realm where dreams have run.

Light and dark in sweet ballet,
Merge and flow, they find their way.
Together in a soft refrain,
Weaving joy from sorrow's pain.

With each stitch, a spark ignites,
Guiding hearts to distant heights.
In shadows deep, we find our way,
A glowing path, come what may.

Stitches of Tomorrow

Each stitch holds a promise dear,
A vision bright that draws us near.
Threads of gold and silver line,
Crafting futures, yours and mine.

Hands that toil with gentle grace,
Sewing dreams in endless space.
Every knot a tale unwinds,
In the fabric, hope we find.

Through the turmoil, through the strife,
We weave the patterns of our life.
With every loop, the past forgives,
In stitches strong, our spirit lives.

Time's embrace can still be kind,
As we stitch the ties that bind.
In the tapestry, futures bloom,
And shadows yield to colors' plume.

Tapestry of Dreams

In the dawn of whispered sighs,
A tapestry beneath the skies.
Colors blend and softly weave,
Crafting dreams that we believe.

Golden threads of morning light,
Stitching visions brave and bright.
Every hue a story told,
In the fabric, futures unfold.

Nightly patterns, rich and deep,
In the silence, secrets keep.
With every stitch, our hearts align,
In the weave, our souls entwine.

Through the struggles, through the fears,
We trace our hopes, we weave our years.
A living quilt, our dreams in flight,
In every heart, a spark of light.

Braided Whispers

Underneath the moon's soft glow,
Braided whispers gently flow.
Voices carried on the night,
Murmurs turning dark to light.

In the silence, stories blend,
Carried forth on breezes' end.
Binding hearts with tales of old,
In their warmth, our dreams unfold.

Threads of laughter, strands of tears,
Weaving tapestries through the years.
Every whisper, every sigh,
Binds us close, we cannot hide.

Through the shadows, through the gleam,
Braided echoes shape our dream.
In this circle, hand in hand,
Whispers braid the life we planned.

Strong Weaves

Threads unite, firm and tight,
Binding stories, day and night,
In the fabric of our lives,
Strength in numbers, harmony thrives.

Hands that labor, hearts that share,
Creating beauty, weaving care,
Colorful patterns, tales to tell,
In every stitch, a dream to dwell.

From frayed edges to vibrant seams,
A tapestry woven from hopes and dreams,
Together we stand, strong and proud,
In the strength of our weaves, we shout loud.

We gather together, generations passed,
In the strong weaves, our bonds will last,
With every thread, we find our place,
In this shared fabric, we find grace.

Beyond the Fabric

Layers of life, a canvas bare,
Beyond the fabric, stories dare,
Dreams that shimmer in the light,
Woven wishes take their flight.

In every fold, a secret lies,
Moments trapped beneath the skies,
Unseen patterns start to weave,
Beyond the fabric, we believe.

Textures blend, and colors speak,
A language found in hearts unique,
Finding solace in the seams,
Beyond the fabric, we chase dreams.

Threads will tangle, but they'll unite,
In the chaos, there's beauty bright,
Expanding beyond the touch and feel,
In every stitch, our truth reveals.

The Color of Tomorrow

Brush strokes bright, palette expands,
The color of tomorrow in our hands,
Painting futures with hope and care,
A vibrant world waiting to share.

Shades of dreams in swirling hues,
Each one a path, a choice to choose,
Daring to create the life we crave,
Coloring hope, the world we save.

Underneath the sun's warm gaze,
We sketch the future, unapologize,
With every tone, a brand new start,
The color of tomorrow fills the heart.

Let the canvas speak our truth,
Of dreams ignited in the youth,
With every brush, we write our song,
The color of tomorrow, bold and strong.

Woven Echoes

In the silence, echoes ring,
Woven whispers, softly sing,
Memories caught in threads of time,
A tapestry rich, a dance in rhyme.

Voices linger, tales entwined,
In every weave, the past aligned,
Fading echoes, yet they stay,
In woven patterns, guiding our way.

Threads connect, a bond we feel,
In these echoes, truths reveal,
Stories shared and lives embraced,
In woven echoes, love is placed.

Together we rise, hand in hand,
A chorus sung across the land,
In every thread, our essence flows,
In woven echoes, life bestows.

The Embrace of Aspirations

In shadows cast by hopes aflame,
We rise anew, pursue the same.
Each whisper stirs the quiet night,
A dance of dreams, a guiding light.

With every step, we carve our way,
Through tangled paths, come what may.
Our hearts aligned, we seek to find,
The purpose held in dreams entwined.

Through trials faced, we stand as one,
Embracing all we've yet to shun.
Together in this sacred flight,
A tapestry of pure delight.

So let the winds of fortune blow,
With open hearts, we shall bestow.
A chorus sung of strength and grace,
In aspirations' warm embrace.

Light Between the Weaves

In the loom of life, threads interlace,
Creating patterns, a subtle grace.
In shades of hope and whispers bright,
We find the balance, joy, and light.

Every stitch a story laced,
Moments captured, none erased.
In the fibers, secrets hold,
A warmth that never will grow cold.

As colors blend, the beauty shows,
With each heartbeat, the tapestry grows.
A symphony of light we weave,
Through every thread, we dream and believe.

Let love be woven, pure and free,
In every corner, intricacy.
Together we shine, a radiant beam,
In the light between the weaves we dream.

Stitching Dreams Together

With needle's point and thread so fine,
We craft our lives, our hopes align.
In every stitch, a dream takes flight,
A quilt of visions, pure and bright.

Gathered close in hearts we share,
Finding strength in those who care.
Through trials faced, we mend the fray,
Stitching dreams that find their way.

Every patch a tale to tell,
Of laughter, love, where hope does dwell.
A tapestry of hearts combined,
In woven threads, our fates entwined.

So let us craft with gentle hands,
A future bright, as hope demands.
Together we find, in each endeavor,
The art of stitching dreams forever.

Tapestry of Tomorrow

In the fabric of time, we weave today,
Stitching a future in our own way.
With threads of courage, colors bold,
We shape a tale, our stories told.

Glimmers of hope in every seam,
We dance together, weaving a dream.
Through trials faced, our spirits soar,
In the tapestry of forevermore.

Let love be the thread that guides our hand,
In the journey ahead, let us stand.
For each knot tied holds a tale of grace,
In this masterpiece, we find our place.

Together we forge what's yet to come,
In harmony's song, our hearts become.
A tapestry bright, stitched with care,
The fabric of tomorrow, ours to share.

Frayed Edges

Threads unravel, whispers fade,
Tales of old in shadows laid.
With every stitch, a story told,
A tapestry of dreams, once bold.

Ripped and worn, still holding tight,
In daylight's grace, they seek the light.
Frayed edges meet the dawn's embrace,
Transformation finds its rightful place.

Through the tears, new colors show,
Embracing change, we learn to grow.
The past a guide, not a chain,
In every loss, there's much to gain.

From frayed to whole, the journey bends,
A quilt of life, where time transcends.
In every stitch, our hopes align,
A dance of hearts, a thread divine.

New Beginnings

In the dawn's soft golden glow,
A whisper stirs, a gentle flow.
The past retreats, the future gleams,
Awaken now to vibrant dreams.

With every step, a breath of chance,
In the unknown, we find our dance.
Seeds of hope, in hands outspread,
From soil's grip, new futures tread.

Together we can paint the sky,
Colors bright and spirits high.
Turning pages, hearts ignite,
In new beginnings, we take flight.

Let go the fear, embrace the grace,
In every moment, love's embrace.
Where every ending clears the way,
To brighter paths that gently sway.

Interwoven Dreams

Threads of silver, strands of gold,
In the loom of fate, we unfold.
Crafting hopes from fears and schemes,
Life's a quilt of interwoven dreams.

Together stitched, through time and space,
Each pattern holds a warm embrace.
In shadows deep, our visions weave,
A tapestry that we believe.

Every knot, a tale to share,
In tangled paths, we find our care.
As colors blend, our spirits beam,
Creating life from shared esteem.

Reaching out through night's embrace,
Finding light in every trace.
In woven dreams, we find our way,
Through intertwined hearts, come what may.

Fabric of New Beginnings

Woven threads of chance and fate,
In life's fabric, we create.
Every stitch a choice we make,
In the quilt of dreams, we awake.

Draped in warmth, we feel the glow,
In every fold, new paths to show.
Patterns shift, designs evolve,
In each embrace, our fears dissolve.

The echoes call, the stitches hum,
In harmony, our spirits drum.
With open hearts, we start anew,
With threads of hope, our dreams pursue.

Each dawn a gift, a canvas bright,
In layers deep, we seek the light.
In the fabric's weave, we find a song,
In new beginnings, we all belong.

Invisible Chains of Hope

Bound by dreams, yet free to soar,
Invisible chains that we explore.
In silent strength, we lift our voice,
Through whispered winds, we make our choice.

Shadows stretch, but light breaks through,
Chains of hope, in colors hue.
In every heart, a hopeful spark,
Guiding us through the shadows dark.

We wear the chains with grace and pride,
In unity, we turn the tide.
With every pulse, our spirits blend,
In invisible chains, we transcend.

Together bound, yet soaring high,
In dreams we trust, we learn to fly.
Through trials faced, our spirits cope,
In every heart, there lies our hope.

Tying Dreams to Reality

In shadows where the whispers flow,
A vision sparks, begins to grow.
Roots of hope in the fertile ground,
With each step, new paths are found.

Bridges made with threads of light,
Weaving visions into night.
What we seek will come to be,
When dreams embrace reality.

Hands outstretched, we chase the dawn,
With hearts alive, we carry on.
Through trials faced and lessons learned,
Each flicker waits, a candle burned.

Tying dreams with strings of fate,
Building futures, never late.
In the tapestry so grand,
Together we will always stand.

Tints of Tomorrow's Glow

A canvas sprawled with colors bright,
Each hue a whisper, pure delight.
Blushing reds and golden yellows,
Paint the dreams of all the fellows.

The morning light begins to spill,
Promising wonders, hope to fill.
With every stroke, the world we make,
Tints of tomorrow that won't break.

Hopeful greens of nature's trees,
Refreshing breaths in gentle breeze.
In every shade, a story told,
Of dreams unfurling, brave and bold.

Together we paint the days ahead,
With vivid visions being spread.
On this palette, life will flow,
In every tint of tomorrow's glow.

The Warp of Endless Possibilities

In the thread of time, we weave,
Stories hidden, hearts believe.
Infinite paths stretch far and wide,
Seeking glimpses of the other side.

Each choice a twist, a turn to share,
In the fabric of dreams, we dare.
Unraveled tapestries, rich and grand,
Within our grasp, futures expand.

The warp and weft, a dance so free,
Embracing all that we might be.
With hopeful hearts and spirits strong,
We'll craft our song, where we belong.

The endless weave, a tale spun bright,
In every stitch, the spark of light.
Through countless choices, we will find,
A world alive, beautifully designed.

Fabrics of Renewal

In the quiet dawn, we mend and sew,
Stitching pieces of life's flow.
Threads of silver, hints of gold,
Fabrics of strength, stories bold.

With every rip, a lesson learned,
In gentle hands, the future turned.
Colors blend, a fresh beginning,
In the dance of life, we're winning.

Embracing change with open hearts,
Rekindling flames, refreshing starts.
In the patterns of our days,
Renewal whispers in myriad ways.

Together we weave, a brave new page,
With love and hope, we disengage.
Fabrics of renewal gather near,
In unity, we hold what's dear.

The Weft of Tomorrow

Threads of dreams, softly spun,
In the quiet, their journey begun.
With each stitch, a vision takes flight,
Weaving the dawn from the depths of night.

Colors blend in a tapestry bright,
Futures crafted by hands in light.
Each moment a loop, every choice a seam,
Together we build, together we dream.

Hope Woven in Silence

In whispers soft, hope does arise,
With quiet strength, it paints the skies.
Stitches sewn with tender care,
A quiet promise drifts in the air.

Each moment held in gentle embrace,
Silent courage, a steadfast grace.
Though storms may come, we stand our ground,
In the stillness, our strength is found.

Strands of Courage

Woven tight in a fabric bold,
Strands of courage, stories told.
Fear may linger, but hearts will rise,
In every thread, fierce spirit lies.

With hands entwined, we face the fight,
Guided by dreams and the stars' soft light.
Together we weave a future bright,
Filling the void with radiant light.

The Cloth of New Horizons

A canvas stretched beneath the sun,
New horizons, journeys begun.
In every fold, a tale unfolds,
Of paths uncharted and treasures untold.

The fabric of life, ever-changing,
With every heartbeat, rearranging.
We join our threads in vibrant array,
Crafting a dawn, embracing the day.

Weaving Light in Shadows

In the hush of twilight's embrace,
Shadows dance with grace.
Threads of hope intertwine,
Illuminating the spine.

Each flicker tells a tale,
Of courage that won't pale.
We gather, strong and bright,
Weaving light in shadows' night.

Silent whispers in the dark,
Ignite the tiniest spark.
Together we forge ahead,
With every word unsaid.

When dawn breaks, dreams arise,
Painting laughter in the skies.
Embracing what we become,
In shadows, we find the sun.

Fabric of Resilience

In stitches of time, we mend,
Worn seams that never bend.
Each thread a story recites,
Of battles, hopes, and fights.

Colors blend in unity,
Weaving strength, setting free.
Through storms and whispered fears,
Our resilience conquers years.

Textures rough, yet tender too,
A tapestry of me and you.
With every loop and twine,
We find our hearts align.

In the fabric's gentle sway,
We discover the light of day.
Bound together, hand in hand,
In resilience, we firmly stand.

Knots of Possibility

Tied in loops, the future waits,
Unraveling through open gates.
Every knot, a chance to see,
Infinite paths waiting to be.

Beneath the weight of binding ties,
Lies potential that never dies.
With each pull and gentle tug,
We feel the warmth, the loving hug.

Twisting dreams in colors bright,
Crafting visions, painting light.
Through the chaos, we will find,
The knots of love, forever blind.

Each connection tells a tale,
Guiding us when we unveil.
In the dance of what may be,
Knots of possibility set us free.

Amongst the Frayed Edges

Amongst the frayed edges, we roam,
Finding solace in the unknown home.
Whispers flutter like autumn leaves,
In the spaces where heart believes.

Tears woven into the threads of time,
Echoing in life's quiet rhyme.
Yet in the wear, there's grace anew,
As we gather strength from what we grew.

Patchwork moments, memories sewn,
In the seams, our stories grown.
Through rugged paths, we see the light,
Amongst the frayed edges, we unite.

Each tear a mark of love so real,
Binding us with a shared feel.
Amongst the flaws, we find our way,
Together we'll seize the day.

Weaving Whispers

In the quiet hours of night,
Whispers blend in soft delight.
Threads of dreams begin to weave,
Silent secrets we believe.

Gentle waves of hope arise,
Underneath the starlit skies.
With each heartbeat, stories spin,
Woven tales that live within.

Voices echo through the dark,
Leaving traces, like a mark.
In the fabric of our minds,
Whispers linger, life unwinds.

Flickers of Tomorrow

In the dawn of morning's glow,
Flickers dance, a vibrant show.
Hope ignites with each new ray,
Guiding dreams to find their way.

Within the shadows, visions spark,
Illuminating paths so stark.
Whispers promise what may be,
Flickers of sweet certainty.

Tomorrow beckons, softly near,
As today fades, no need for fear.
In the light, our spirits rise,
Flickers shining in our eyes.

Tapestry of Light

Woven strands of shining gold,
Stories waiting to be told.
In the fabric of the night,
Every thread a spark of light.

Colors dance in harmony,
Creating patterns wild and free.
In each knot, a moment caught,
Tapestry of dreams we sought.

Glimmers twine in careful weave,
Through the dark, our hearts believe.
Crafted by hands that care,
Woven visions, bright and rare.

Twinkling Threads

Like stars that grace the velvet sky,
Twinkling threads that flutter by.
In the cosmos, tales unfold,
Stories whispered, dreams retold.

Each twinkle paints a memory bright,
Guiding wanderers through the night.
Connected paths, though far apart,
Twinkling threads bind every heart.

In the silence, love will bloom,
Chronicles bathed in silver moon.
Threads entwined, a fateful dance,
Twinkling bright, our souls' romance.

Milton Keynes UK
Ingram Content Group UK Ltd.
UKHW020043271124
451585UK00012B/1028

This book is part of a captivating poetry book series that journeys through the ethereal realms of dreams and the quiet intimacy of bedtime. Each book, written by a different author, brings a unique voice to the timeless themes of sleep, imagination, and the mysteries of the night. From lullabies that soothe the soul to dreamscapes filled with wonder and whimsy, the series captures the delicate moments when reality slips away and the mind begins to wander.

ISBN 978-9916-90-825-9